T0124063

Website

Username

Password

Notes

⬦ ⬦ ⬦ ⬦ ⬦ ⬦

Website

Username

Password

Notes

⬦ ⬦ ⬦ ⬦ ⬦ ⬦

Website

Username

Password

Notes

A

Website

Username

Password

Notes

◇ ◇ ◇ ◇ ◇ ◇

Website

Username

Password

Notes

◇ ◇ ◇ ◇ ◇ ◇

Website

Username

Password

Notes

Website _____

Username _____

Password _____

Notes _____

_____

_____

_____

Website _____

Username _____

Password _____

Notes _____

_____

_____

_____

◇ ◇ ◇ ◇ ◇ ◇

"The next time you think of beautiful things, don't forget to count yourself among them!"

A

Website

Username

Password

Notes

◇ ◇ ◇ ◇ ◇ ◇

Website

Username

Password

Notes

◇ ◇ ◇ ◇ ◇ ◇

Website

Username

Password

Notes

Website

Username

Password

Notes

◇ ◇ ◇ ◇ ◇ ◇

Website

Username

Password

Notes

◇ ◇ ◇ ◇ ◇ ◇

Website

Username

Password

Notes

*"Wake up grateful, and
watch how the day unfolds."*

◇ ◇ ◇ ◇ ◇ ◇

Website

Username

Password

Notes

◇ ◇ ◇ ◇ ◇ ◇

Website

Username

Password

Notes

Website

Username

Password

Notes

◇ ◇ ◇ ◇ ◇ ◇

Website

Username

Password

Notes

◇ ◇ ◇ ◇ ◇ ◇

Website

Username

Password

Notes

B

Website

Username

Password

Notes

◇ ◇ ◇ ◇ ◇ ◇

Website

Username

Password

Notes

◇ ◇ ◇ ◇ ◇ ◇

Website

Username

Password

Notes

C

Website

Username

Password

Notes

◇ ◇ ◇ ◇ ◇ ◇

Website

Username

Password

Notes

◇ ◇ ◇ ◇ ◇ ◇

Website

Username

Password

Notes

C

Website
Username
Password
Notes

◇ ◇ ◇ ◇ ◇ ◇

Website
Username
Password
Notes

◇ ◇ ◇ ◇ ◇ ◇

Website
Username
Password
Notes

C

Website

Username

Password

Notes

◇ ◇ ◇ ◇ ◇ ◇

Website

Username

Password

Notes

◇ ◇ ◇ ◇ ◇ ◇

Website

Username

Password

Notes

Website

Username

Password

Notes

◇ ◇ ◇ ◇ ◇ ◇

Website

Username

Password

Notes

◇ ◇ ◇ ◇ ◇ ◇

Website

Username

Password

Notes

Website _____

Username _____

Password _____

Notes _____

_____

_____

_____

◇ ◇ ◇ ◇ ◇ ◇

Website _____

Username _____

Password _____

Notes _____

_____

_____

_____

◇ ◇ ◇ ◇ ◇ ◇

Website _____

Username _____

Password _____

Notes _____

_____

_____

_____

Website _____

Username _____

D

Password _____

Notes _____

_____

_____

_____

"Fabric doesn't ask questions. Fabric understands!"

Website _____

Username _____

Password _____

Notes _____

_____

_____

_____

Website _____

Username _____

Password _____

Notes _____

_____

_____

_____

◇ ◇ ◇ ◇ ◇ ◇

Website _____

Username _____

Password _____

Notes _____

_____

_____

_____

◇ ◇ ◇ ◇ ◇ ◇

Website _____

Username _____

Password _____

Notes _____

_____

_____

_____

D

Website

Username

Password

Notes

◇ ◇ ◇ ◇ ◇ ◇

Website

Username

Password

Notes

◇ ◇ ◇ ◇ ◇ ◇

Website

Username

Password

Notes

Website

Username

Password

Notes

E

◇ ◇ ◇ ◇ ◇ ◇

Website

Username

Password

Notes

◇ ◇ ◇ ◇ ◇ ◇

Website

Username

Password

Notes

E

Website

Username

Password

Notes

◇ ◇ ◇ ◇ ◇ ◇

Website

Username

Password

Notes

◇ ◇ ◇ ◇ ◇ ◇

Website

Username

Password

Notes

Website _____

Username _____

Password _____

Notes _____

_____

_____

_____

E

◇ ◇ ◇ ◇ ◇ ◇

Website _____

Username _____

Password _____

Notes _____

_____

_____

_____

◇ ◇ ◇ ◇ ◇ ◇

Website _____

Username _____

Password _____

Notes _____

_____

_____

_____

E

Website

Username

Password

Notes

◇ ◇ ◇ ◇ ◇ ◇

Website

Username

Password

Notes

◇ ◇ ◇ ◇ ◇ ◇

Website

Username

Password

Notes

Website

Username

Password

Notes

F

◇ ◇ ◇ ◇ ◇ ◇

Website

Username

Password

Notes

◇ ◇ ◇ ◇ ◇ ◇

Website

Username

Password

Notes

F

Website

Username

Password

Notes

◇ ◇ ◇ ◇ ◇ ◇

Website

Username

Password

Notes

◇ ◇ ◇ ◇ ◇ ◇

Website

Username

Password

Notes

"In a world where you can be anything, be yourself."

◇ ◇ ◇ ◇ ◇ ◇

Website

Username

Password

Notes

_____

_____

_____

◇ ◇ ◇ ◇ ◇ ◇

Website

Username

Password

Notes

_____

_____

_____

F

Website

Username

Password

Notes

◇ ◇ ◇ ◇ ◇ ◇

Website

Username

Password

Notes

◇ ◇ ◇ ◇ ◇ ◇

Website

Username

Password

Notes

Website

Username

Password

Notes

◇ ◇ ◇ ◇ ◇ ◇

Website

Username

Password

Notes

◇ ◇ ◇ ◇ ◇ ◇

Website

Username

Password

Notes

G

G

Website

Username

Password

Notes

◇ ◇ ◇ ◇ ◇ ◇

Website

Username

Password

Notes

◇ ◇ ◇ ◇ ◇ ◇

Website

Username

Password

Notes

Website

Username

Password

Notes

◇ ◇ ◇ ◇ ◇ ◇

Website

Username

Password

Notes

◇ ◇ ◇ ◇ ◇ ◇

Website

Username

Password

Notes

Website

Username

Password

Notes

◇ ◇ ◇ ◇ ◇ ◇

Website

Username

Password

Notes

◇ ◇ ◇ ◇ ◇ ◇

Website

Username

Password

Notes

Website

Username

Password

Notes

◇ ◇ ◇ ◇ ◇ ◇

Website

Username

Password

Notes

◇ ◇ ◇ ◇ ◇ ◇

Website

Username

Password

Notes

*"Life's a boomerang—
what you give, you get!"*

H

◇ ◇ ◇ ◇ ◇ ◇

Website

Username

Password

Notes

◇ ◇ ◇ ◇ ◇ ◇

Website

Username

Password

Notes

Website _____

Username _____

Password _____

Notes _____

_____

_____

_____

◇ ◇ ◇ ◇ ◇ ◇

Website _____

Username _____

Password _____

Notes _____

_____

_____

_____

◇ ◇ ◇ ◇ ◇ ◇

Website _____

Username _____

Password _____

Notes _____

_____

_____

_____

H

Website

Username

Password

Notes

◇ ◇ ◇ ◇ ◇ ◇

Website

Username

Password

Notes

◇ ◇ ◇ ◇ ◇ ◇

Website

Username

Password

Notes

Website

Username

Password

Notes

◇ ◇ ◇ ◇ ◇ ◇

Website

Username

Password

Notes

◇ ◇ ◇ ◇ ◇ ◇

Website

Username

Password

Notes

Website

Username

Password

Notes

I

◇ ◇ ◇ ◇ ◇ ◇

Website

Username

Password

Notes

◇ ◇ ◇ ◇ ◇ ◇

Website

Username

Password

Notes

Website

Username

Password

Notes

◇ ◇ ◇ ◇ ◇ ◇

J

Website

Username

Password

Notes

◇ ◇ ◇ ◇ ◇ ◇

Website

Username

Password

Notes

J

Website _____

Username _____

Password _____

Notes _____

_____

_____

_____

◇ ◇ ◇ ◇ ◇ ◇

Website _____

Username _____

Password _____

Notes _____

_____

_____

_____

◇ ◇ ◇ ◇ ◇ ◇

Website _____

Username _____

Password _____

Notes _____

_____

_____

_____

Website _____

Username _____

Password _____

Notes _____

_____

_____

_____

◇ ◇ ◇ ◇ ◇ ◇

Website _____

Username _____

Password _____

Notes _____

_____

_____

_____

◇ ◇ ◇ ◇ ◇ ◇

Website _____

Username _____

Password _____

Notes _____

_____

_____

_____

K

Website

Username

Password

Notes

◇ ◇ ◇ ◇ ◇ ◇

K

Website

Username

Password

Notes

◇ ◇ ◇ ◇ ◇ ◇

Website

Username

Password

Notes

Website _____

Username _____

Password _____

Notes _____

_____

_____

_____

K

"I understand the concept of cooking and cleaning ... just not how it applies to quilters!"

Website _____

Username _____

Password _____

Notes _____

_____

_____

_____

Website

Username

Password

Notes

◇ ◇ ◇ ◇ ◇ ◇

K

Website

Username

Password

Notes

◇ ◇ ◇ ◇ ◇ ◇

Website

Username

Password

Notes

Website _____

Username _____

Password _____

Notes _____

_____

_____

_____

◇ ◇ ◇ ◇ ◇ ◇

Website _____

Username _____

Password _____

Notes _____

_____

_____

_____

◇ ◇ ◇ ◇ ◇ ◇

Website _____

Username _____

Password _____

Notes _____

_____

_____

_____

L

Website

Username

Password

Notes

◇ ◇ ◇ ◇ ◇ ◇

Website

Username

Password

Notes

◇ ◇ ◇ ◇ ◇ ◇

Website

Username

Password

Notes

Website _____

Username _____

Password _____

Notes _____

_____

_____

_____

◇ ◇ ◇ ◇ ◇ ◇

Website _____

Username _____

Password _____

Notes _____

_____

_____

_____

◇ ◇ ◇ ◇ ◇ ◇

Website _____

Username _____

Password _____

Notes _____

_____

_____

_____

L

Website

Username

Password

Notes

◇ ◇ ◇ ◇ ◇ ◇

L

Website

Username

Password

Notes

◇ ◇ ◇ ◇ ◇ ◇

Website

Username

Password

Notes

Website

Username

Password

Notes

◇ ◇ ◇ ◇ ◇ ◇

Website

Username

Password

Notes

M

◇ ◇ ◇ ◇ ◇ ◇

Website

Username

Password

Notes

Website

Username

Password

Notes

◇ ◇ ◇ ◇ ◇ ◇

Website

Username

Password

Notes

◇ ◇ ◇ ◇ ◇ ◇

Website

Username

Password

Notes

Website _____

Username _____

Password _____

Notes _____

_____

_____

_____

◇ ◇ ◇ ◇ ◇ ◇

Website _____

Username _____

Password _____

Notes _____

_____

_____

_____

M

◇ ◇ ◇ ◇ ◇ ◇

Website _____

Username _____

Password _____

Notes _____

_____

_____

_____

Website

Username

Password

Notes

◇ ◇ ◇ ◇ ◇ ◇

M

Website

Username

Password

Notes

◇ ◇ ◇ ◇ ◇ ◇

Website

Username

Password

Notes

Website

Username

Password

Notes

◇ ◇ ◇ ◇ ◇ ◇

Website

Username

Password

Notes

N

◇ ◇ ◇ ◇ ◇ ◇

Website

Username

Password

Notes

Website _____

Username _____

Password _____

Notes _____

_____

_____

_____

◇ ◇ ◇ ◇ ◇ ◇

Website _____

Username _____

Password _____

Notes _____

_____

_____

_____

N

◇ ◇ ◇ ◇ ◇ ◇

"Laughter is life's sweetest creation. Go on! Laugh out loud!"

Website

Username

Password

Notes

◇ ◇ ◇ ◇ ◇ ◇

Website

Username

Password

Notes

◇ ◇ ◇ ◇ ◇ ◇

Website

Username

Password

Notes

Website _____

Username _____

Password _____

Notes _____

_____

_____

_____

◇ ◇ ◇ ◇ ◇ ◇

Website _____

Username _____

Password _____

Notes _____

_____

_____

_____

◇ ◇ ◇ ◇ ◇ ◇

Website _____

Username _____

Password _____

Notes _____

_____

_____

_____

N

Website

Username

Password

Notes

◇ ◇ ◇ ◇ ◇ ◇

Website

Username

Password

Notes

O

◇ ◇ ◇ ◇ ◇ ◇

Website

Username

Password

Notes

Website

Username

Password

Notes

◇ ◇ ◇ ◇ ◇ ◇

Website

Username

Password

Notes

O

◇ ◇ ◇ ◇ ◇ ◇

Website

Username

Password

Notes

Website _____

Username _____

Password _____

Notes _____

_____

_____

_____

◇ ◇ ◇ ◇ ◇ ◇

Website _____

Username _____

Password _____

Notes _____

_____

_____

_____

P

◇ ◇ ◇ ◇ ◇ ◇

Website _____

Username _____

Password _____

Notes _____

_____

_____

_____

Website

Username

Password

Notes

◇ ◇ ◇ ◇ ◇ ◇

Website

Username

Password

Notes

P

◇ ◇ ◇ ◇ ◇ ◇

Website

Username

Password

Notes

"Simply begin. Anywhere."

◇ ◇ ◇ ◇ ◇ ◇

Website

Username

Password

Notes

Q

◇ ◇ ◇ ◇ ◇ ◇

Website

Username

Password

Notes

Website

Username

Password

Notes

◇ ◇ ◇ ◇ ◇ ◇

Website

Username

Password

Notes

Q

◇ ◇ ◇ ◇ ◇ ◇

Website

Username

Password

Notes

Website _____

Username _____

Password _____

Notes _____

_____

_____

_____

◇ ◇ ◇ ◇ ◇ ◇

Website _____

Username _____

Password _____

Notes _____

_____

_____

_____

◇ ◇ ◇ ◇ ◇ ◇

R

Website _____

Username _____

Password _____

Notes _____

_____

_____

_____

Website

Username

Password

Notes

◇ ◇ ◇ ◇ ◇ ◇

Website

Username

Password

Notes

R

◇ ◇ ◇ ◇ ◇ ◇

Website

Username

Password

Notes

Website _____

Username _____

Password _____

Notes _____

_____

_____

_____

◇ ◇ ◇ ◇ ◇ ◇

Website _____

Username _____

Password _____

Notes _____

_____

_____

_____

◇ ◇ ◇ ◇ ◇ ◇

S

Website _____

Username _____

Password _____

Notes _____

_____

_____

_____

Website

Username

Password

Notes

◇ ◇ ◇ ◇ ◇ ◇

Website

Username

Password

Notes

◇ ◇ ◇ ◇ ◇ ◇

S

Website

Username

Password

Notes

Website _____

Username _____

Password _____

Notes _____

_____

_____

_____

◇ ◇ ◇ ◇ ◇ ◇

Website _____

Username _____

Password _____

Notes _____

_____

_____

_____

◇ ◇ ◇ ◇ ◇ ◇

Website _____

Username _____

Password _____

Notes _____

_____

_____

_____

S

Website

Username

Password

Notes

◇ ◇ ◇ ◇ ◇ ◇

Website

Username

Password

Notes

◇ ◇ ◇ ◇ ◇ ◇

S

Website

Username

Password

Notes

Website _____

Username _____

Password _____

Notes _____

_____

_____

_____

◇ ◇ ◇ ◇ ◇ ◇

Website _____

Username _____

Password _____

Notes _____

_____

_____

_____

◇ ◇ ◇ ◇ ◇ ◇

T

"There are no mistakes *in quilting ... only* pot holders!"

Website

Username

Password

Notes

◇ ◇ ◇ ◇ ◇ ◇

Website

Username

Password

Notes

◇ ◇ ◇ ◇ ◇ ◇

T

Website

Username

Password

Notes

Website _____

Username _____

Password _____

Notes _____

_____

_____

_____

◇ ◇ ◇ ◇ ◇ ◇

Website _____

Username _____

Password _____

Notes _____

_____

_____

_____

◇ ◇ ◇ ◇ ◇ ◇

Website _____

Username _____

Password _____

Notes _____

_____

_____

_____

Website

Username

Password

Notes

◇ ◇ ◇ ◇ ◇ ◇

Website

Username

Password

Notes

◇ ◇ ◇ ◇ ◇ ◇

Website

Username

Password

Notes

Website _____

Username _____

Password _____

Notes _____

_____

_____

_____

◇ ◇ ◇ ◇ ◇ ◇

Website _____

Username _____

Password _____

Notes _____

_____

_____

_____

◇ ◇ ◇ ◇ ◇ ◇

Website _____

Username _____

Password _____

Notes _____

_____

_____

_____

U

Website

Username

Password

Notes

◇ ◇ ◇ ◇ ◇ ◇

*"Surround yourself with people
who encourage you to blossom!"*

◇ ◇ ◇ ◇ ◇ ◇

U

Website

Username

Password

Notes

Website

Username

Password

Notes

◇ ◇ ◇ ◇ ◇ ◇

Website

Username

Password

Notes

◇ ◇ ◇ ◇ ◇ ◇

Website

Username

Password

Notes

V

Website

Username

Password

Notes

◇ ◇ ◇ ◇ ◇ ◇

Website

Username

Password

Notes

◇ ◇ ◇ ◇ ◇ ◇

Website

Username

Password

V Notes

Website _____

Username _____

Password _____

Notes _____

_____

_____

_____

◇ ◇ ◇ ◇ ◇ ◇

Website _____

Username _____

Password _____

Notes _____

_____

_____

_____

◇ ◇ ◇ ◇ ◇ ◇

Website _____

Username _____

Password _____

Notes _____

_____

_____

_____

W

Website

Username

Password

Notes

◇ ◇ ◇ ◇ ◇ ◇

Website

Username

Password

Notes

◇ ◇ ◇ ◇ ◇ ◇

Website

Username

Password

Notes

W

Website _____

Username _____

Password _____

Notes _____

_____

_____

_____

◇ ◇ ◇ ◇ ◇ ◇

Website _____

Username _____

Password _____

Notes _____

_____

_____

_____

◇ ◇ ◇ ◇ ◇ ◇

Website _____

Username _____

Password _____

Notes _____

_____

_____

X

_____

Website

Username

Password

Notes

◇ ◇ ◇ ◇ ◇ ◇

Website

Username

Password

Notes

◇ ◇ ◇ ◇ ◇ ◇

Website

Username

Password

Notes

X

*"Gather the threads of your life,
and stitch them into joy!"*

◇ ◇ ◇ ◇ ◇ ◇

Website

Username

Password

Notes

◇ ◇ ◇ ◇ ◇ ◇

Website

Username

Password

Notes

Y

Website _____

Username _____

Password _____

Notes _____

_____

_____

_____

◇ ◇ ◇ ◇ ◇ ◇

Website _____

Username _____

Password _____

Notes _____

_____

_____

_____

◇ ◇ ◇ ◇ ◇ ◇

Website _____

Username _____

Password _____

Notes _____

_____

_____

_____

Y

Website _____

Username _____

Password _____

Notes _____

_____

_____

_____

◇ ◇ ◇ ◇ ◇ ◇

Website _____

Username _____

Password _____

Notes _____

_____

_____

_____

◇ ◇ ◇ ◇ ◇ ◇

Website _____

Username _____

Password _____

Notes _____

_____

_____

_____

Z

Website _____

Username _____

Password _____

Notes _____

_____

_____

_____

◇ ◇ ◇ ◇ ◇ ◇

Website _____

Username _____

Password _____

Notes _____

_____

_____

_____

◇ ◇ ◇ ◇ ◇ ◇

Website _____

Username _____

Password _____

Notes _____

_____

_____

_____

Z